Insects In Quran
The Locust
Samy Mahdy
AF480582
Insects In Quran

1

Samy Mahdy

Insects in Quran

Children Handbook

3 - Locust.

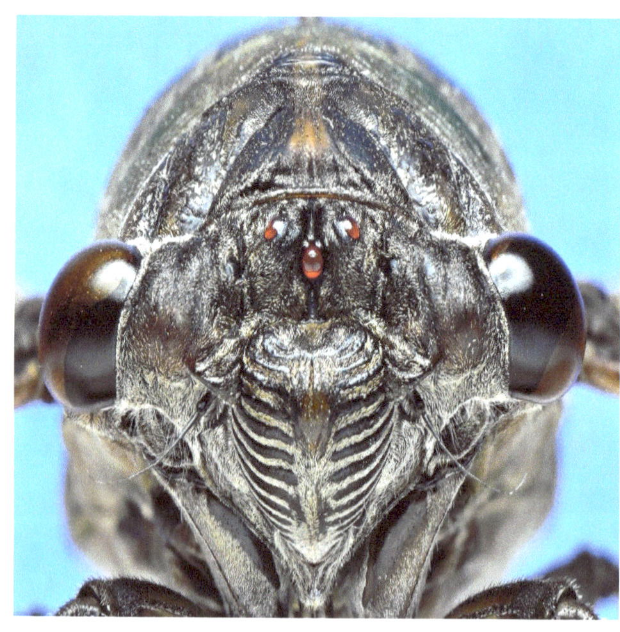

Samy Mahdy

There are ten insects mentioned in Holy Quran:

1- Ants

2 - Bees

3- Locust

4 - Flies

Samy Mahdy

5 -Spider

6 - Mosquitos

7 - Lice

8 - Butterflies

9 - Termit

10 - Bugs

Samy Mahdy

Locust mentioned in the Holy Quran in (2) times:

1. So We sent upon them the flood, and the locusts, and the lice, and the frogs, and the blood, detailed verses, so they were

arrogatting and were a criminal kinsfolk.7:133

2 - Their sights are humbled, they are exiting from the burial sites, as if they were spreading locusts.54:07

Locust Life Cycle:

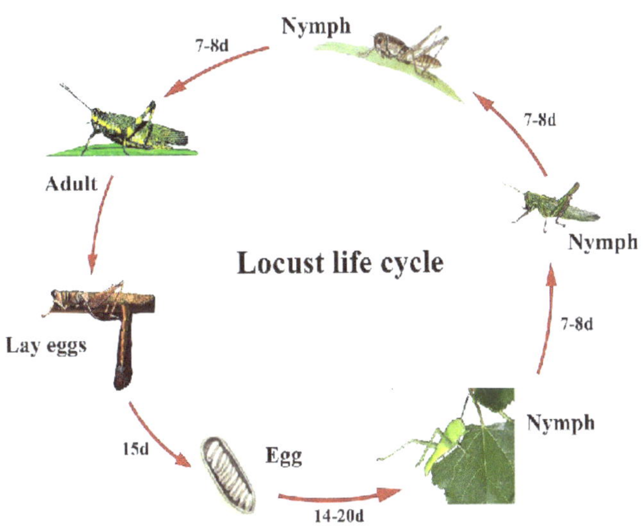

Some Locust Types:

Samy Mahdy

The Biggest Locust size.

Short-horned=11cm

The smallest Locust size.

Small Locust =7-10 mm

The Most Dangerous Locust

The Desert Grasshopper

Locust History In Quran:

1 - Allah told Moses that He will send the Locust as one of nine verses over Egypt. The locusts covered the face of the land and swallowed up every crop and all the fruits of the trees. Afterwards there was nothing green in the trees, and all the crops in the fields had been destroyed.

2 - On the resurrection day the people will exit out from burial sites, as if they were spreading locusts coming out from their breeding nests.

Mention Three Types of Locust:

1 -

2 -

3 -

Play

Samy Mahdy

The Locust

Paint

Samy Mahdy

Let us know

Difference between
Grasshopper & Mantis

1 - Praying mantis are related to grasshoppers, crickets, roaches and katydids. They belong to an order of insects called Orthoptera.

2 - Mantis have enormous appetites, eating various aphids, leafhoppers, mosquitoes, caterpillars and other soft-bodied insects when young. Later they will eat larger insects, beetles, grasshoppers, crickets, and other pest insects.

Locust Communication

The mating behavior of the desert locust. Before mating, males actively scanned the visual field, frequently cleaned their antennae and compound eyes, and jumped toward the females. The females, in response, moved slowly in front of the males and vibrated their entire bodies. These studies affirm, for the first time, the emission of a sex pheromone by the solitarius females that attracts males.

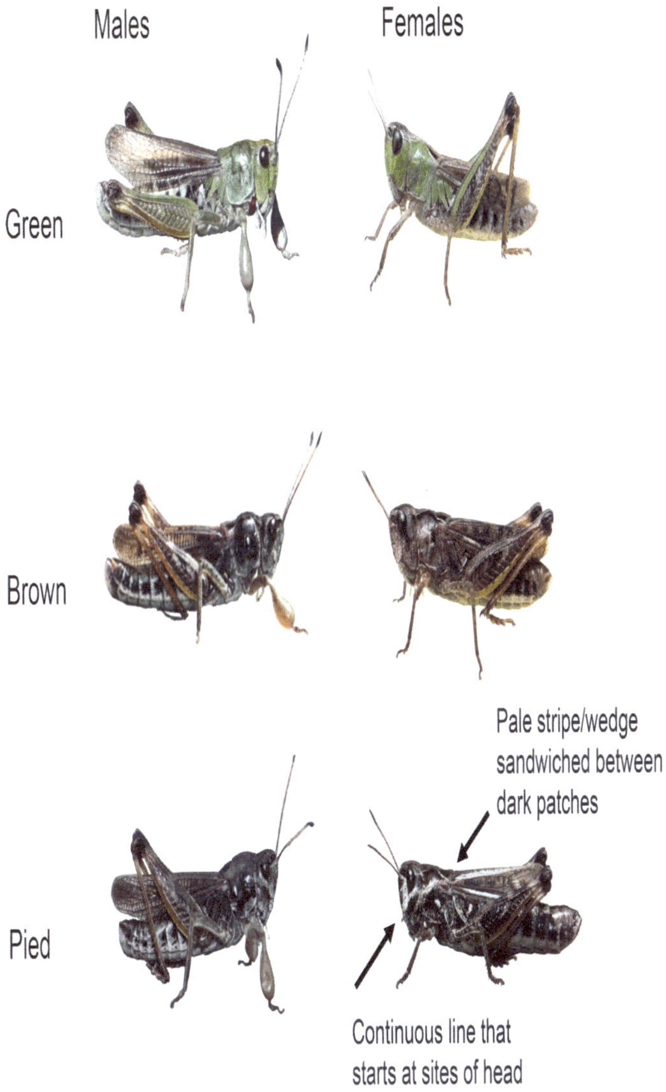
Males
Females
Green
Brown
Pied
Pale stripe/wedge sandwiched between dark patches
Continuous line that starts at sites of head

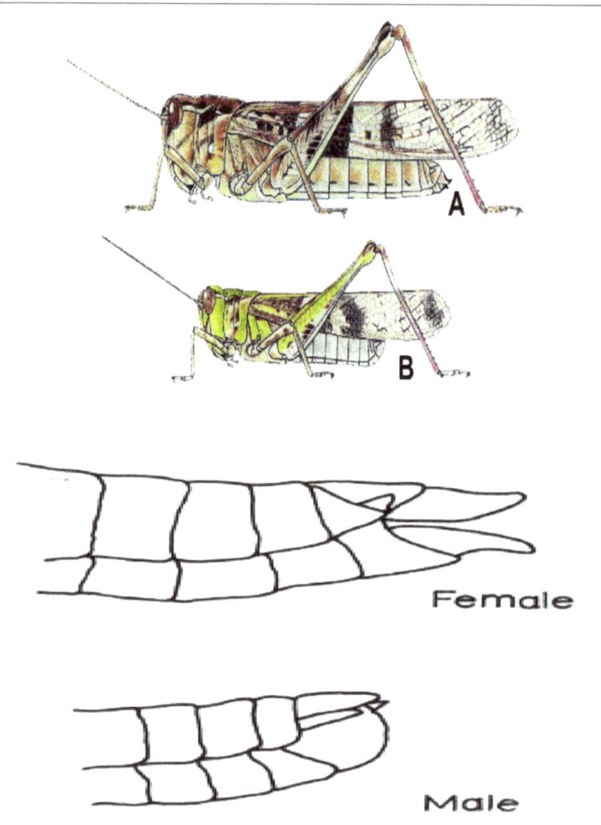

A – Female

B – Male

Table of contents